WORLD OF SPORTS

SAILING

Published by Smart Apple Media
123 South Broad Street, Mankato, Minnesota 56001

Photography: cover, pages 3, 8, 17, 19—CORBIS/Neil Rabi-
nowitz; pages 7, 21, 25, 27, 29—CORBIS/Nick Rains; Cordaiy
Photo Library, Ltd.; pages 9, 23—CORBIS/Johnathan Smith;
Cordaiy Photo Library, Ltd,; pages 10, 11, 26, 28, 30—
CORBIS/Roger Ressmeyer; page 15—CORBIS/The Mariner's
Museum; page 18—CORBIS/Betmann; page 22—CORBIS/
Layne Kennedy

Design and Production by EvansDay Design

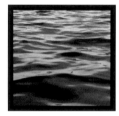

LIBRARY OF CONGRESS CATALOGING-IN-PUBLICATION DATA

Bach, Julie S., 1963–
Sailing / by Julie Bach.
p. cm. — (World of sports)
Includes index.
Summary: Presents some of the history, equipment, com-
petitors, and competitions in the sport of sailboat racing.
ISBN 1-887068-58-9
1. Sailing—Juvenile literature. 2. Yacht racing—Juvenile
literature. [1. Sailboat racing. 2. Sailing.] I. Title. II. Series:
World of sports (Mankato, Minn.)
GV811.B23   2000
797.1'24—dc21   98-36406

First edition
9   8   7   6   5   4   3   2   1

SAILING

JULIE BACH

*At the equator, there were starry nights
and glass and useless breezes too feeble
to dry sweat or raise a hair. . . . To coax
what little air there was, Browne had
raised a ghoster jib, a big light sail with
a Kevlar luff sheeted to the afterdeck.
He spent hours looking over the stern,
watching the little mill-pond ripple of
the current under his keel. The water
was crazy blue, painted, Brazilian.*

OUTERBRIDGE REACH

by Robert Stone

A Sailing Adventure

■———■

THE CHAMPIONSHIP RACE is about to begin. The fleet of sailboats has been whittled down race after race, and only two remain. Finishing off the best-of-seven competition between finalists, the two sailboats jockey for position behind the starting line. They **tack** around each other again and again, their bright sails contrasting with the dark blue water. Huge crowds watch from the shore or from boats anchored near the starting line. The sailors are tense and quiet, but the crowds are in a cheering mood. The crews on the boats can hear their shouts and whistles.

The closest finish in an America's Cup race occurred on October 4, 1901. The British boat Shamrock II *crossed the finish line just two seconds ahead of the American boat* Columbia. *However, the American crew went on to win the Cup.*

The starting gun goes off. Crew members quickly set their sails to catch the wind, and the contest begins. It's a fine day for sailing: the wind is steady but not too strong, the seas are not too high, and the sun is bright. Many of the sailors wear a thick paste of white sunscreen on their noses to prevent sunburn.

The American **yacht** gains the advantage at the starting line and takes the lead. The two sailboats head out to the ocean, aiming for a **buoy** that marks the first turn. Every so often, the American **skipper** shouts, "Tacking!" and turns the steering wheel. As the boat turns in a new direction, the enormous **boom** sweeps across the deck. Crew members duck their heads to avoid being knocked into the ocean.

Paul Elvstrom of Denmark won a record four Olympic gold medals in sailing—one each in 1948, 1952, 1956, and 1960. He was also the first competitor to win individual gold medals in four successive Olympics.

When the skipper tacks, the rest of the crew leaps into action. Several sailors wind up the **sheets** that control the sails. Others jump to the side of the boat and lay down on the edge, leaning as far out over the water as

tack *a method of turning a sailboat to keep the sails full of wind*

yacht *a large sailboat designed for racing*

buoy *a float that marks a place in the water*

A SAILBOAT CREW WORKS FURIOUSLY TO KEEP ITS LEANING YACHT UPRIGHT IN STRONG WAVES.

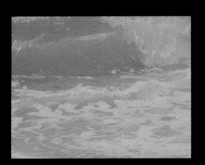

skipper *the person who steers the boat and directs the crew*

boom *a horizontal beam attached to the mast that holds the mainsail*

sheets *ropes used to control the sails*

they can, to keep the boat balanced. The **mainsail** leans far to the other side. The enormous force of the wind pushes the boat along the surface of the waves.

The sailors on board feel the spray of ocean water and the freshness of the wind. They hear the shouts of other crew members as everyone works together to stay in the lead. No one rests for a moment. Racing a large boat is a complicated and demanding task that requires speed, strength, perfect timing, and a bit of intuition.

The Americans are still in the lead as the boats round the final mark, a large yellow buoy. Both boats are now sailing with the wind instead of tacking against it. The skipper shouts. In response, crew members raise the spinnaker, a sail

at the front of the boat that will catch the full power of the wind. As soon as that sail is up, the other one comes down.

Now both boats race at top speed across the water. At times, they sail so close together that they seem about to collide. During the race, the seas have grown higher. With each swell, the **bow** of the American yacht rises high in the air, then falls with a thud back into the sea. The race becomes an adventure in speed, spray, and risk. The gloved hands of the crew members strain at the ropes and sails. One wrong move could cost the Americans the race.

ITS FRONT SAIL FILLED BY A STIFF BREEZE, AN AMERICA'S CUP SAILBOAT GLIDES ACROSS THE DARK BLUE OCEAN.

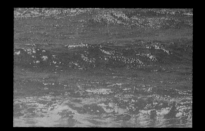

mainsail *the largest sail on a boat that has several sails*

bow *the front of a boat*

As the two competitors approach the finish line, the Americans maintain a slight lead. Their boat is taking full advantage of the wind. When the yacht crosses the finish line, the gun goes off again, marking the end of the race. Spectators *The fastest speed ever recorded by a sailing yacht is 36.2 knots (42 miles per hour or 67.6 km/h). Jean Saucet of France set this record in his boat,* Charante Maritime, *on October 5, 1992.* on nearby boats cheer, wave flags, and celebrate the victory. Once again, the Americans have won the most prestigious sailboat race in the world—the America's Cup.

THE CREW OF THE 39-FOOT (12 M) SAILBOAT *USA* TESTS THE YACHT'S STABILITY IN HIGH SEAS IN THE SAN FRANCISCO BAY.

Sailing through History

THE SWIFT, LIGHTWEIGHT sailboats of today are descendants of boats that people built thousands of years ago. No one knows exactly when the first sail was made, but **hieroglyphics** on Egyptian vases indicate that sails were in use by 3000 B.C. Some historians think sails existed 1,000 years before that.

The sail became one of the most important inventions in the history of human civilization. With sailboats, people could reach faraway lands they would otherwise never see. They could transport goods and settle in new places.

The Scandinavians, the Cretans, and the Phoenicians were among the best early sailors. In the ninth century, Vikings, who came from what is now Norway, Sweden, and Denmark, became the first people to build boats with a **keel**. This strong, straight piece of wood ran the length of the bottom of a boat,

The longest nonstop sailing race in the world is the Vendeé Globe Challenge, which was first run in 1989. Frenchman Christophe Auguin holds the record for the fastest time on the 22,500-mile (36,203 km) course: 105 days, 20 hours, and 31 minutes. This time is also the record for the fastest solo sailing trip around the world.

making the craft stronger and more stable. After that invention, little changed in sailing until the 20th century.

About 2,000 years ago, the Phoenicians voyaged to the island of Britain, introducing the square sail there. Hundreds of years later, the English would assemble the best and largest sailing fleet in the world. In fact, Great Britain ruled the high seas by the 19th century, controlling a vast empire largely through the force of its sailing fleet.

In 1851, England invited other countries to participate in a sailboat race. The queen offered a silver cup worth 100 guineas as the winner's prize. Because Britain was the world's foremost naval power, everyone assumed that an English ship would win the race.

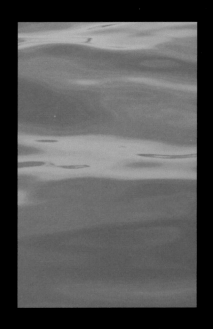

THE TOWERING MASTS OF BIG SAILBOATS MUST BE WELL-BALANCED AND STURDY ENOUGH TO WITHSTAND VERY STRONG WINDS.

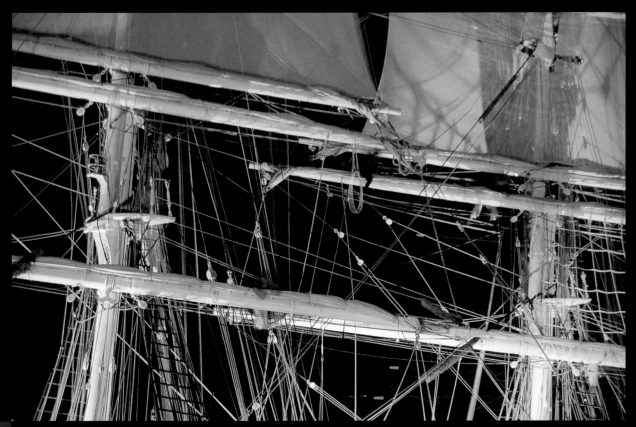

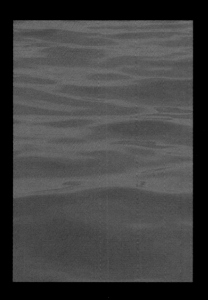

hieroglyphics *a form of picture writing used by ancient Egyptians*

keel *the horizontal beam that gives structure to the hull*

schooner *a fast, two-masted ship with a narrow hull*

The **schooner** *America* sailed to the Isle of Wight, where the race would be held. Sponsored by the New York Yacht Club, *America* was the best and fastest boat the United States had to offer.

England's King Charles II is credited with owning the first real yacht, the Mary, *in the 17th century.*

The sailboat race covered 50 miles (80.5 km) and took 10 and a half hours to complete. To everyone's surprise, the American schooner finished first. The New York Yacht Club took home the silver cup and kept it in a place of honor. Both the cup and the race became known as the America's Cup. *America*'s victory in 1851 signaled the beginning of the end of Britain's dominance of the oceans.

Soon after its victory, the New York Yacht Club announced that it would accept challenges for the America's Cup. England tried to win back the Cup for the next several decades. Races were held every three to four years, but an American ship won every time. In fact, the United States successfully defended the Cup for an incredible 132 years.

The New Face of Racing

TODAY, THERE ARE two types of sailboat races. In a **regatta**, many boats race against one another at the same time. In a **match race**, only two boats race at a time. The America's Cup combines both types and has become the pinnacle of sailboat racing. The boats are the best in the world, the sailors are skilled, and the competition is intense. Men and women may spend years of their lives training for this race.

Captain Joshua Slocum earned fame in 1898 when he completed the first solo trip around the world in a sailboat. The journey took him three years. He is considered the grandfather of all solo sailors.

The America's Cup is held whenever the current winner invites challengers. Any boat from any country can challenge as long as it meets the specifications decided on by a committee that oversees the race. Dozens of boat crews from around the world pay hefty entrance fees. During months of competition, races called "trials" are run, and boats are gradually eliminated. Finally, only one challenger remains. That challenger competes in a best-of-seven series of match races against the current champion.

For a long time, sailboat racing was a "gentlemen's" sport. Only people with a great deal of money could afford the large wooden boats with heavy cloth sails. The vessels were typically raced by men only.

Then, in the 1950s, manufacturers began making boats out of **fiberglass**, a strong material invented during World War II. Fiberglass revolutionized sailing by making boats lighter, stronger, and easier to maintain. It also made them cheaper. More people could afford to buy a boat, and sailing became a pastime for people from all income brackets.

Hope Goddard Iselin was the first woman to sail in an America's Cup final race. She was the timekeeper on Defender in 1895.

In the world of racing, builders who used fiberglass could create sailboat designs that had not been possible with wood. Many of the new designs made racing boats lighter, narrower, and faster. Unfortunately, the

A YACHT'S SKIPPER TURNS THE HELM, OR STEERING WHEEL, AS HE SURVEYS THE COURSE AHEAD.

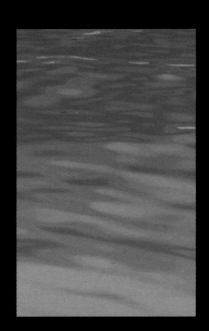

regatta   *a sailboat race between many boats*

match race   *a sailboat race between two boats*

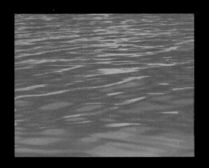

designs also made the boats less stable. During the 1960s and '70s, sailboat racing was plagued by disasters as boats capsized and sailors drowned. Boat designers seemed willing to sacrifice safety for speed.

In recent years, designers and racing organizations have begun returning to the stable **hull** designs of the past. British designer Edward Burnett has been flooded with orders for his old-style boats. "If you had told me a year ago that this would happen, I would have laughed in disbelief," Burnett said. Many sailing fans hope that sailboat racing will again become a sport that puts safety first.

Boats and Crews

—

THERE ARE MANY sizes and styles of sailboats. Any boat with one hull is called a monohull boat. A catamaran has two narrow hulls joined by strong beams. A catboat has one sail. A sailing dinghy is a small, open catboat. Boats that have two or more sails include sloops, yawls, ketches, cutters, and schooners.

To ensure even competitions, sailboat racers developed the International Offshore Rule (IOR). This is a system used to rate boats based on their length, breadth, weight, and sail area. Boats are rated A (biggest) to E (smallest), and the faster boats are assigned handicaps to make the competition fair.

Phyllis Brodie Gordon Sopwith and Gertie Vanderbilt are two of only three women to have sailed in an America's Cup final. Both women sailed as timekeepers with their husbands in the 1934 and 1937 races.

A big sailboat may require a racing crew of 12 or more members. The skipper, or **helmsman**, is in charge, steering the boat and directing the crew. The **tactician** is second in importance, advising the skipper on strategy. Sailing strategy includes deciding which sails to use, when to

A SAILOR—HOISTED HIGH INTO THE AIR— SECURES A GIANT SAIL DURING A YACHT RACE ACROSS LAKE SUPERIOR.

pass other boats, and when to tack. Other crew members include watchmen, navigators, and pitmen. One crew member has the duty of climbing the **mast** and repairing or securing the sails if necessary.

Sailing depends entirely on the wind. If a boat is sailing with the wind, its sails are set out to the sides to catch the full force of the breeze. If a boat is sailing against the wind, it must tack back and forth, using the wind to move it for-

helmsman *another name for the skipper or captain of a sailboat*

tactician *the crew member who advises the skipper on strategy*

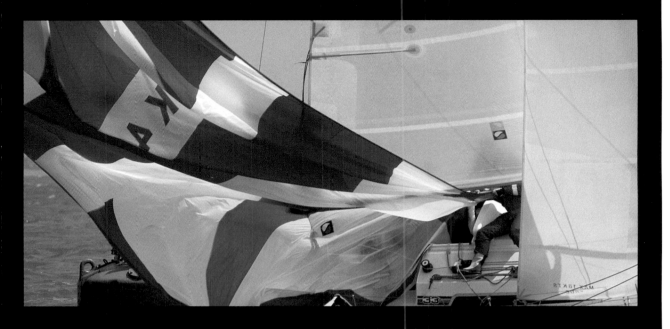

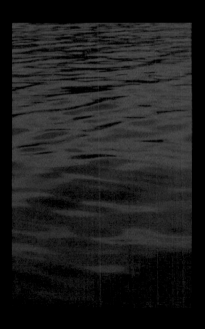

mast *the tall pole that rises from the center of the boat and to which sails are attached*

stern *the back of the boat*

ward. The sails are set at an angle to the wind, which moves the boat first to the right, then to the left, but always forward.

Beginning sailors must learn the proper terms for parts of a sailboat. The bow is the front end of the boat, and the **stern** is the back end. **Port** means the side of a boat that is on the left as a person faces the bow, and **starboard** refers the right side. Sailboats have a vertical **centerboard**, or daggerboard, that extends into the water like the fin of a fish; it stabilizes the boat and keeps it from tilting. Boats also have a **rudder** for steering.

The mast rises from the middle of the boat. Sailors attach the sails to the mast and to the boom, a horizontal pole that sticks out from the mast. Ropes attached to the sails are called sheets, and the sheets are tied to metal brackets called **cleats**.

Ninety-mile-per-hour (150 km/h) winds and 35-foot (10.5 m) waves turned the 1998 Sydney-to-Hobart yacht race into a disaster. The annual Australian race, which begins the day after Christmas, ended with the deaths of six sailors and the sinking of seven boats.

Rugged Racers

■ ▭ ■

SAILBOAT RACERS ARE an adventurous and often colorful group, particularly those who compete in the America's Cup. One of the most famous American skippers is Ted Turner, owner of television networks and the Atlanta Braves baseball team. Turner won the America's Cup in 1977 in his boat *Courageous*, beating experienced Australian skipper Alan Bond.

Donald Crowhurst attempted one of the greatest frauds in sports history when he faked his voyage around the world in the Golden Globe race. He drifted in the South Atlantic while calling in false position reports. Months after the race ended, his boat was found drifting in the mid-Atlantic, and Crowhurst was never seen again.

The sport of sailboat racing changed when Turner began competing in the 1970s. Before he started winning, ocean competitions were more like leisurely cruises than races. Crews shortened their sails at night in order to sleep. Boats were stocked with extra food supplies and comfortable furniture.

Turner won by pushing his crews 24 hours a day. He stripped his boats of unnecessary furniture and other luxuries to make them lighter.

His crews trained full-time rather than part-time to become the best sailors in the field. Turner's crews were virtually invincible until other skippers learned from his example and started beating him at his own game.

Turner was a Southerner in a sport dominated by Easterners, and for a while, he was not accepted by the upper-class yachting establishment.

In 1993, Hugo Vihlen became the world-record holder for crossing the Atlantic Ocean in the smallest boat, sailing across the North Atlantic in a five-foot, four-inch (162 cm) boat named Father's Day.

But his colorful personality, outspokenness, and confidence brought new energy to the sport of sailing. Throughout the '70s, Americans who had never seen a sailboat race became interested in the sport after seeing Turner interviewed on television. The talented skipper drew a great deal of atten-

No matter how large the sailboat, any venture on the ocean can be risky when the wind whips up huge waves.

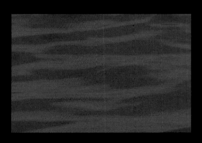

port *the left side of a boat as a person faces the bow*

starboard *the right side of a boat as a person faces the bow*

centerboard *a board that hangs from the bottom of the hull and stabilizes a sailboat*

tion to the America's Cup and to sailboat racing in general. Turner retired from the sport in 1981 after racing boats such as *American Eagle, Lightning, Vamp X,* and *Tenacious.*

Turner's successor was Dennis Conner, one of the biggest names in sailboat racing. Although he won the America's Cup three times, he may be best-remembered as the first American skipper ever to *lose* the America's Cup. This blow to the American racing community came in 1983, when Conner lost to an Australian boat. It was the first America's Cup ever televised live, so viewers throughout the world witnessed Conner's defeat.

But Conner had never been one to give up, and in 1987, he went "down under" for a rematch with the Australians. In a remarkable comeback performance, he swept the first four races of the best-of-seven series and reclaimed the Cup. The event was again televised, and people everywhere watched Conner win the fourth race, a victory that made him a minor celebrity. He sailed for the San Diego Yacht Club, so when the cup was returned to the United States, it was kept in San Diego rather than New York.

Unfortunately for the United States, Conner lost the America's Cup again in 1995—this time to New Zealand. Many U.S. teams were lining up to win it back in the year 2000.

SAILING CREWS PUT IN MANY LONG, HARD HOURS OF PRAC- TICE TOGETHER TO PREPARE FOR THE AMERICA'S CUP AND OTHER BIG RACES.

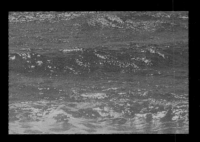

rudder *a device at the back of a*
boat that is used for steering

cleats *metal brackets around*
which ropes are tied

Dawn Riley of Detroit, Michigan, is one of the few women who have competed in America's Cup trials, which determine who will run in the final races. Riley was on the crew of the *America3* during the 1992 trials. In 1995, she was part of the first all-female crew ever to enter the America's Cup, again sailing on *America3.*

Riley has also competed in a famous race called the Whitbread Round-the-World Race. Held every few years, this race covers 31,600 miles (50,844 km). Competitors sail all the way around the world, but the race is staged in "legs," or sections, so the racers get a few breaks. The entire race takes about four months. Riley was the skipper of an all-women's team in the 1993–94 Whitbread race.

In 1997–98, skipper Paul Cayard

In December 1994, during an around-the-world solo race called the BOC Challenge, French sailor Isabelle Autissier was nearly lost at sea when a huge wave rolled her boat completely over. Autissier survived for three days in an air pocket inside the boat before a helicopter rescued her.

won the Whitbread by a large margin in a yacht called *EF Language.* "It is hard to summarize the whole race right now," he said after winning. "What I can say for sure is that it has been the most unusual and exceptional sporting experience of my life. Winning is just the icing on the cake."

Although Cayard was born in San Francisco, he raced for an Italian sailing organization for years. In 1998, he was mounting his first American-based challenge for the America's Cup, hoping to compete in the race in the year 2000. But sailors stay busy even in the years between America's

Cup races. Members of the 1,200 yachting clubs in the United States can race on local, regional, and national levels. Some of the top crews may compete in global races, overseen by the International Yacht Racing Union. The pinnacle of small-craft racing, though, is the Olympic Games. In 2000, sailing was to be a medal event in the Games at Sydney, Australia, for the first time. Pre-trial regattas to prepare for the Olympic Games began years in advance of the event.

Perhaps the most grueling sailboat race anywhere is the Around Alone, in which one person races a sailboat on a route around the world, covering a distance of about 27,000 miles (43,443 km). There's no crew—just the skipper. The solo race was first staged in 1982–83, and it has since become very popular. Many competitors who begin the grueling competition cannot finish the race; some boats capsize, and some sailors become sick or simply give up. A French competitor named Isabelle Autissier became the first woman to ever finish the

In 1969, Sharon Sites Adams became the first woman to make a solo crossing of the Pacific Ocean. She sailed from Japan to San Francisco, a distance of 5,620 miles (9,043 km), in 74 days, 17 hours, and 15 minutes.

BEHIND THE GRACEFUL
APPEARANCE OF A
LARGE, CRUISING SAIL-
BOAT IS THE STRENUOUS
AND OFTEN DRENCHING
WORK OF ITS CREW.

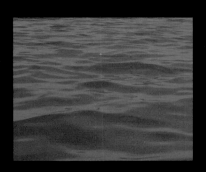

SMALL SAILBOATS FOR ONE OR
TWO PASSENGERS ARE A PEACE-
FUL WAY TO ENJOY THE WATERS
OF SMALLER LAKES OR THE
COASTLINES OF THE OCEAN.

Around Alone, finishing seventh in her class in 1990–91.

Today, sailing has become a popular pastime throughout the world, with more than 100,000 new sailors taking to the water each year. Many enjoy leisurely trips in cruise boats, preferring to vacation rather than race. Their boats are often equipped with all the comforts of home, including stoves, refrigerators, beds, and toilets.

But the sailors who compete in such races as the America's Cup, the Whitbread, and the Around Alone are rugged souls who dedicate themselves to the sport of sailboat racing. It takes strength, dedication, and skill. Like the sailors of long ago, they spend much of their lives on the water, doing what they love best.